# Survival

## Could You Be An OTTER ?

**Photography – Fiona Pragoff**
**Illustrations – Dee Morgan**
**Natural History and expert tips –**
**Roger Tabor**

The rules of the Game:

■ Each time you turn the page, you score **SURVIVAL** points.

✗ When you've achieved your best score, you can challenge your friends to see if they can beat you.

**IDEALS CHILDREN'S BOOKS**
Nashville, Tennessee

Start Here

Scramble up the bank and go exploring? Go to 4

Dive into the river and see what's wriggling? Go to 6

You've just woken up from an early morning nap and are feeling very hungry. Right beneath you something is wriggling in the water – if you're quick, you may catch it. But what else is happening? You sniff the air to test the wind. Something smells good just up the bank. Wait – there's an eel caught in that net staked out in the river. That's a tasty meal. Which way will you go? You are poised for action. What you decide could mean a healthy meal – or it could mean disaster, even death. Choose now.

**Go for the eel in the net?**
**Go to 9**

Y ou've been swimming fast without catching anything. Now you need a rest. You settle in the warm shallows, your nose continually testing the air. It seems safe here. It's a good time to go up the bank and groom your coat. That's always fun, and it keeps your fur warm and waterproof. Some insects flick across the surface of the water. Everything is peaceful. Why not relax and catch your breath?

**Relax in the shallows?**
**Go to 3**

Climb up the
bank and
groom your
coat?
Go to 4

2

Explore the
pipe?
Go to 19

**+ 5 Points**

Hunting further along the bank, you come face to face with a motorboat heading fast downstream. With powerful engines throbbing and propellers thrashing the water, it seems as if it is rushing angrily to attack you. No time for thought, only escape. Two ways are open to you: swim under the footbridge toward the town or push through the reeds to the bank. Quick, decide!

**3**

Under the
footbridge?
Go to 14

Through the
reeds to the
bank?
Go to 17

+ 8 Points

As you clamber along the bank, a fat, juicy frog hops right in front of you. Frogs are one of your special treats, and you crunch it up quickly – delicious! Are there any more here? Maybe in the meadow? You look around and spot one of your favorite places – a mud slide down the bank into the river. That's always fun. But what's that stirring in the reeds? More food? Or something more dangerous? Which way do you go?

See what's in the reeds? Go to 3

**4**

Go hunting in
the meadow?
Go to 13

Skid down the
mud slide?
Go to 15

# 5

**— 3 Points**

**D**rowned! Those eels were easy prey, but when you tried to come up for air, you found you could not turn around in the narrow end of the net. Now you're dead. Go back to 1 and start again.

Expert tip
*Fishing nets and lobster traps are a menace to otters. The creatures caught in them are so tempting that otters often swim inside – and then get trapped themselves and drown. Otters will swim into empty nets too purely out of curiosity.*

# 6

**+ 3 Points**

**Y**ou chase after a fat, juicy eel. It gives you a hard swim, but you catch it – a real treat! But the water has turned darker and fouler. Perhaps something is poisoning the river here. Go on to 14.

Expert tip
*Eels can survive in water polluted severely enough to kill most fish, so even badly poisoned waters can provide meals for otters.*

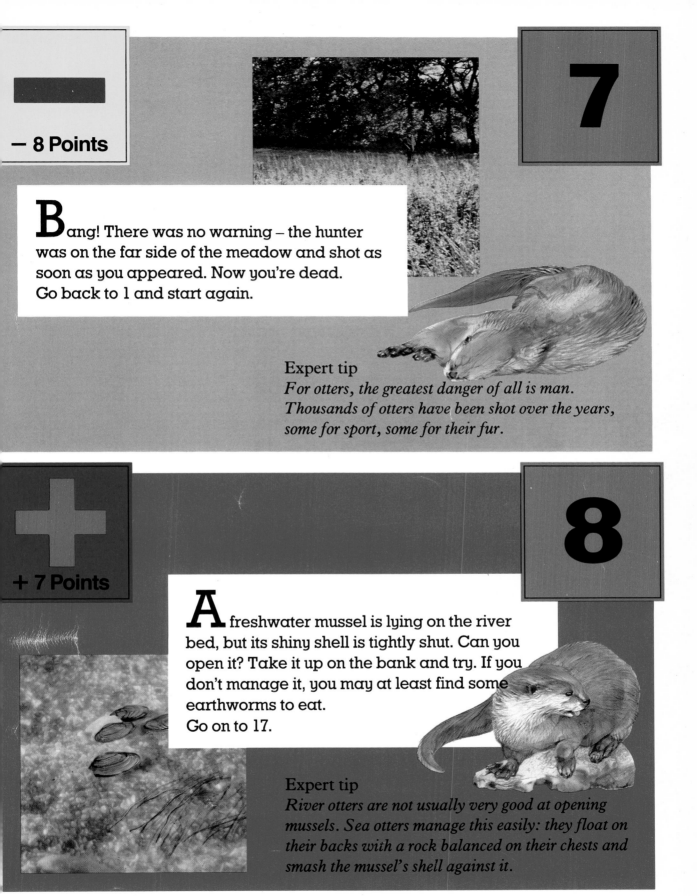

**— 8 Points**

**7**

**B**ang! There was no warning – the hunter was on the far side of the meadow and shot as soon as you appeared. Now you're dead.
Go back to 1 and start again.

Expert tip
*For otters, the greatest danger of all is man. Thousands of otters have been shot over the years, some for sport, some for their fur.*

**+ 7 Points**

**8**

**A** freshwater mussel is lying on the river bed, but its shiny shell is tightly shut. Can you open it? Take it up on the bank and try. If you don't manage it, you may at least find some earthworms to eat.
Go on to 17.

Expert tip
*River otters are not usually very good at opening mussels. Sea otters manage this easily: they float on their backs with a rock balanced on their chests and smash the mussel's shell against it.*

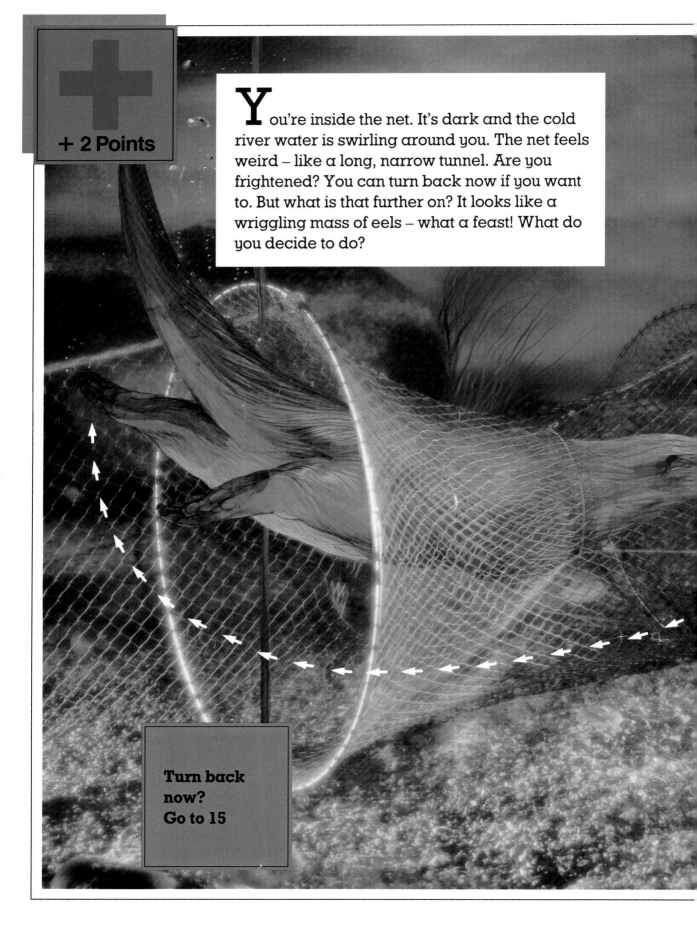

+ 2 Points

You're inside the net. It's dark and the cold river water is swirling around you. The net feels weird – like a long, narrow tunnel. Are you frightened? You can turn back now if you want to. But what is that further on? It looks like a wriggling mass of eels – what a feast! What do you decide to do?

Turn back now?
Go to 15

**9**

Go for the
eels?
Go to 5

# 10

**+ 8 Points**

**Y**our high speed chase took you quickly through the dangerous chemicals, but now the water is becoming white and soapy, and the oil that protects your fur is washing off. The water is getting straight through to your skin. You begin to shiver with cold. Quick – look for a place to land and dry out.
Go to 2.

Expert tip
*Otters need to groom their coats to keep them warm and waterproof. Detergents dissolve the covering of oil on their fur and let the water reach their skin. They can die of cold from this.*

# 11

**+ 4 Points**

**Y**ou were fast – but the trout was faster. Now you're out of breath and still hungry. Perhaps you should have chosen the minnows. Too late now, they've gone!
Give yourself the chance to find something else to eat.
Go to 8.

Expert tip
*Trout can swim extremely fast, so otters normally chase slower fish such as minnows.*

**— 15 Points**

**12**

**Y**ou didn't see the car until far too late – and the driver never saw you at all. He was sorry, but you are dead.
Go back to 1 and start again.

Expert tip
*Many otters are killed on the roads. You might expect them to keep to the water, but they travel on land too. Males especially travel a lot – normally 3 miles a night and often much more.*

**— 10 Points**

**13**

**F**rom where you were, you couldn't quite see the dog, and it took you unaware. You never had a chance, and now you're dead.
Go back to 1 and start again.

Expert tip
*Over the centuries, man has used dogs to hunt otters. Happily, any hunting of otters is now illegal or strictly regulated in most of North America.*

+ 5 Points

An easy
catch?
Go to 18

The water by this factory stinks and it tastes horrible. All the same, there are fish around. That one to your right is going so slowly, it would be an easy catch. And there's another, smaller fish shooting very fast upstream. Which do you choose?

**A fast chase?**
**Go to 10**

**15**

**S**wimming powerfully upstream once more, you pause for a moment on a patch of pebbles. That slide was fun, but now you are hungry again. You spot something unusual nowadays – a crayfish near the surface of the water. Crayfish are tasty, but those pincers can hurt! You look around. Up the bank on the edge of a marsh, a tiny duckling stumbles into view, calling for its mother. It doesn't know how appetizing it looks. Then . . . plop! you hear one of your favorite sounds, the splash of a leaping fish. Is it too far away to catch? Time for a quick decision – what will you do?

**Chase after that fish? Go to 16**

+ 10 Points

Take
a rest?
Go to 23

Chase the
minnows
upstream?
Go to 21

After a hectic chase, you finally lost your fish; but now, suddenly, you are face to face with lots of them. There is a school of minnows to your left and a nice fat trout to your right. They're both the same distance away from you, but swimming in opposite directions. Choose one quickly, or you'll lose them all! Or would you rather just climb up in those roots and take a well-earned rest? Which is it to be?

16

**Chase the trout downstream? Go to 11**

Further upstream, all is quiet sunshine and slow-moving water. Nothing stirs on the bank. You can tell by the feel of your skin that your coat needs grooming; the water is beginning to come through. This looks like a good place to do it. But there's another mud slide into the river – what about some fun first? What's your decision?

Down the slide and have some fun?
Go to 15

# 18

That fish was swimming so slowly because it was barely alive, poisoned by chemicals from the factory. You ate it hungrily, but the fish poisoned you too, and now you're dead.
Go back to 1 and start again.

— 10 Points

Expert tip
*Pollution kills many otters today. Farmers and factories use chemicals which get washed into the rivers and poison the fish. By continuously eating these fish, an otter will die from the buildup of poison in his body.*

# 19

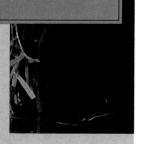

Disaster! The pipe was exciting at first, with lots of frogs to catch and eat. Then the water began to taste funny, poisoned by chemicals from the farm nearby. Later, the food ran out. You pressed on, hoping to find your way out, but there wasn't one. You felt sicker and sicker and now you're dead.
Go back to 1 and start again.

— 8 Points

Expert tip
*It is difficult for otters to find enough food, day after day. Both young and old otters often die of hunger. There are many other dangers too. Only one or two otters out of every hundred live to be 10 years old.*

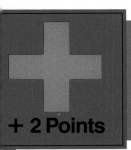

**+ 2 Points**

**T**hat duckling on the edge of the marsh would have eased your hunger pains, but a rat got there before you. The marsh has been drained since you were here last, and now there's nothing for you at all. Move on to 2.

Expert tip
*Marshes are disappearing all over the world as they are reclaimed for building or planting. This means that a large part of the otters' natural habitat is gradually being destroyed.*

**+ 9 Points**

**Y**ou swim faster than little fish, and you caught lots of minnows. Now you're full, and you're getting sleepy. You want to curl up in one of your favorite dens, a deep, warm hollow under the roots of an old willow tree. The river here seems to have moved. It's running faster and straighter – and your willow tree has gone. Now what are you going to do? You need a rest, but your den has been destroyed. You'll have to move on.
Go on to 22.

*Many rivers have been reshaped to suit farmers and other users of the land. Moving the rivers in this way often destroys the otters' homes, which stops them from breeding.*

Swimming easily with the current, after your meal, you come to a fork in the river. The main channel goes straight ahead, but a large dog is barking at a stick in the water. Perhaps you could go around behind him, across the road, and down again on the other side? You could try the smaller channel on the left. That leads to one of your favorite homes, the hole under the old oak tree. Which way would you choose?

Head for home? Go to 23

**22**

Up the bank
and over the
road?
Go to 12